FREE BONUS GIFT

Free Easy-To-Learn Biblical Hebrew Alphabets Learning cards. Please download the bonus gift here: https://larkins.org/hebrewcards

THANK YOU

For purchasing my eBook. In a world that discourages personal revelation which God gives through his Word to his people and with increasing voices like "You cannot interpret the Bible that way".

I want to resolve the confusion and give assurance that you can confidently rest in the Scriptures.

For our, God is not the author of confusion, but peace, as in all churches of the saints. The result is this eBook.

If you have any questions about this book, if you want someone to pray with you or if you just want to talk to someone, please send me a message on WhatsApp at +17477778001 or email me at hello@larkins.org

TABLE OF CONTENTS

ACKNOWLEDGEMENT

I thank Jesus for working in me the desire to work out this book to bear fruit to God. I pray this book will give you the confidence to rest in the perfect word of God.

I would like to thank my sisters in Christ, **Susan Zomparelli** and **Allison Ramirez** without whom this book would have been impossible. They helped me edit the book and keep true to the mission.

They also scolded me when I got lazy while working on the book, some of my feelings were hurt. Nevertheless, the book was completed on time.

INTRODUCTION

The power of life and death. Like nuclear energy, the Bible can bring a massive supply of power, yet in the wrong hands is also able to bring destruction.

The church will experience life when the truth of the grace of Christ is taught, which will cause the church to see a loving Father who sent His son to die on the cross for our sins. But the church experiences death when mortality is taught as the Gospel.

I have been asking God why many people don't understand Grace when it is explained so plainly in the Bible. Though Paul wrote 13 books discussing Law vs Grace, we rarely hear his conclusions being preached in churches.

Here are six ways people read the Bible that lead to wrong believing and end up preaching bad theology:

 1) People see the Bible as a set of rules which causes the Bible to then be portrayed as contradicting rules.

2) The ones who see the Bible as a moral guide. It comes out as biased towards the undeserving.

3) Some try to find science in the Bible but end up finding a lot of scientific errors.

4) Some try to find or make a religion out of The Bible but end up finding death.

5) Those trying to augment their political stance using the bible end up with disappointments.

6) Those who use the bible to condemn other people's sin

or to justify their own sinful lifestyle end up being severely embarrassed.

God spoke to me saying that the Bible is Encrypted with Christ's finished works on the cross as the 'public key', and the discernment of Law vs Grace as the 'private key'.

Use any Keys apart from these and the Word will be grossly misunderstood. A coder or a computer science student would know what these terms mean.

If you have never heard of Encryptions or all the nerdy lingo before don't worry, I have explained in detail the 14 tools you can use to understand the bible better to debunk wrong theologies in this book.

1. VISUALIZATION

Do you remember all the things you imagined you could be one day when you were a child?

Maybe you imagined being an astronaut and going through space discovering planets and having adventures. Or maybe you dreamed of being a doctor while travelling the world and helping the sick.

Now that you have grown up, what happened to those dreams?

Why have we exchanged our beautiful dreams for lesser dreams? Instead, we find that we use our imagination for sex, money, possessions, worthless worries and fear. This is not God's desire for you.

When we read the Bible do, we read to understand the logic behind the verses and try to reason it with the current situation, modern philosophy or morality?

If so, we are doing it wrong. The Bible is not meant to be reasoned by our logic but experienced with our heart's eyes or imagination.

I pray that the eyes of your heart may be enlightened in order that you may know the hope to which He has called you, the riches of His glorious inheritance in His holy people.

~ Ephesians 1:18

God wants us to be like little children. Therefore, the Bible has so many pictures of childlike faith for us to imagine.

Read the Bible and *imagine* the stories happening! See yourself in the events. Revel in all the descriptive accounts of the Bible. Bible events are meant to be imagined!

Above all see your lust, worries and fears being transferred to the Cross; and Christ's righteousness transferring to you.

Then God can replace all those useless thoughts and ambitions. He can fill your mind with innovative ideas that will help mankind.

Ask God to help you visualize the Bible, ask Him to produce images in your mind that activate the childlike imaginations and dreams He has placed within you. With God, you can dare to dream BIG things like a child again.

2. OMIT ITALICS

Have you noticed that some words in the Bible are in *ITALICS*? These were added by translators to conjugate the words for better understanding of sentences.

While translating from one language to another the problem occurs while conjugating sentences and keeping the same meaning. These filler words make it easy to read.

For example:
looking unto Jesus, the author and finisher of *our* faith
~ Hebrews 12:2

The word "our" does not appear in the original Greek. This was added to make the sentence more readable and grammatically correct.

Often these Italic words change the meaning of the entire sentence. It helps us to better understand the original scripture if we omit these Italic words.

For Example:

Jesus therefore, knowing all things that would come upon Him, went forward and said to them, "Whom are you seeking?"
They answered Him, "Jesus of Nazareth."
Jesus said to them, "I am *He.*" And Judas, who betrayed Him, also stood with them. Now when He said to them, "I am *He,*" they drew back and fell to the ground.

~ John 18:4-6

Notice the *He* in "I am *He.*" is in italics and is added. So if you ignore the italic word it becomes "I am". The soldiers who came to arrest Jesus fell to the ground because that's the name of God.

'What *is* His name?' What shall I say to them?"
And God said to Moses, "I AM WHO I AM."

~ Exodus 3:13-15

Remember God the father said "I am" twice? Even Jesus did the same. Omitting italic words gives us tremendous revelations and understanding of the Bible.

3. HEBREW AND GREEK

The Scriptures. Rightly Dividing the Word of truth. Originally written in Hebrew (Old Testament) and Greek (New Testament) leaves us reliant upon the words translated by others. Although a great place to start, we can go deeper, much deeper. Into the recesses of the mind of God and the beauty of His message to us.

To understand the grammar of the original language and its meaning is to know more than simply the English translation. A study of Hebrew and Greek is necessary.

Reading the Biblical text in the original languages identifies the author's emphasis. Alliteration, assonance, poetic structure, chiasm, marked/unmarked word order and the like are usually lost in translation but can and do become clear when reading in the original languages.

Double-check the word and sentences if a certain passage or verse does not make sense. Remember, a text CANNOT mean what the grammar of that text does not support.

Our primary goal is to understand the grammar of the original language, not the grammar of English translation, and for this, we need to know the original Biblical languages.

Ideally, we would all learn Hebrew and Greek but thankfully we can use software like Blue Letter Bible or MySword Bible to help us research in the original languages.

4. HEBRAISM

Hebraism are idioms in the Hebrew language; when the literal meaning of individual words is different from the actual meaning of the whole phrase.

For example, in English, we might say 'they spilt the beans. No beans were spilt. It means someone has told a secret or revealed something prematurely. Another popular one is It's Raining Cats and Dogs. These are idioms.

Hebraism is an expression or construction, distinctive of the Hebrew language, or a Hebraic idiom if you will.

For example, "Holding Snakes and Drinking Poison" (Mark 16:18) means extreme danger, not actual snakes or poison. Another example "Fear and Trembling" is not Trembling with fear But Happy Excitement.

'Flowing with milk and honey', 'stiff-necked' and 'the way of women', are other common Hebraisms found in the Bible.

The study of Hebraism helps us to understand the Biblical culture, Jewish people, their everyday life, national ideology, and culture more clearly.

5. RIGHTLY DIVIDING THE WORD

Everything in the Bible is for our benefit, but not everything written is addressed to *us* as believers.

The Bible addresses each separately to the Jews, the gentiles, the Church, the believer, the Devil and at times specific individuals. Knowing who is speaking, and to whom can make a huge impact on our understanding and our faith.

Some of the biggest heretical theologies are created when everything written in the Bible is thought to be for the Church or the believer.

Study to shew thyself approved unto God, a workman that needeth not to be ashamed, rightly dividing the word of truth.

~ 2 Timothy 2:15

Rightly dividing the word, and discerning to whom the Bible is addressing tears down many bondages created by bad theologies. And the Bible asks us not to be ashamed of it.

One of the largest and most erroneous theologies is about the function of the Holy Spirit. Many myths and crazy theologies surround this topic.

One of the most common misconceptions is that the Holy Spirit convicts us of our sins.

This is a lie and not Biblical.

Let's find out from the Bible;

And when He has come, He will convict the world of sin [people of the world, this is not talking about you], and of righteousness [referring to disciples and also you & me], and of judgment [devil and his works]: of sin, because they do not believe in Me; of righteousness, because I go to My Father and you see Me no more; of judgment, because the ruler of this world is judged.

~ John 16:8-11

NOTICE Jesus is addressing 3 people in this verse, the world, disciples and the devil. The Holy Spirit convicts the World of only <u>one</u> sin, the sin of *unbelief* in Jesus. Believers, on the other hand, are those who have accepted Christ and His finished works, whom the Holy Spirit convicts of their righteousness n Christ Jesus. Judgment is reserved for Satan.

It's very interesting to note that the Holy Spirit *DOES NOT* convict the world of Homosexuality, drug abuse, prostitution, drunkenness, listening to music or appreciating fashion. The Holy Spirit convicts the world of only ONE sin: *Unbelief in Jesus Christ.*

The Holy Spirit convicts believers of righteousness even when we sin (Yes we all sin let's not act all holy and mighty) because of Jesus' finished work on the cross.

God sees Jesus' perfect works instead of us because he is our High Priest. And if the high priest is pure and blameless, so are we in this world.

Some may find it heretical to rightly divide and apply the word because tradition and religion have taught them to apply the *entire* Bible to themselves.

Don't let your former beliefs and traditions shame you from rightly dividing the Word.

Rightly dividing the word does not stop at identifying to whom the bible is referring to but goes further with discerning Law vs Grace and different Dispensations which I have explained in the following chapters.

6. LAW VS GRACE

Much of the Christian world does not like Paul's teaching. His letters are the constitution of the Christian faith, and yet many twists the teachings to support their man-made theology.

People cannot comprehend the awesome light found in Law versus Grace, the 10 commandments versus Jesus, or The Tree of Knowledge of Good and Evil versus The Tree of Life, so they end up balancing Paul's words with their understanding and theology.

"I only read the portion written in red" is a common phrase among religious Christians today. They are saying that they ONLY recognise the words of Jesus as scripture.

Paul boldly explains that the 10 commandments are the power of sin and that we ought to be dead to the 10 commandments, but many Christians cannot handle this truth.

The light is too bright. The easiest way out would be to go back to the dispensation before the finished work of Jesus on the cross and put Christ's words above Paul's. Many Christians seem to forget that the letters of Paul *are* the words of our risen Christ.

Peter has something to say about this:

Our beloved brother Paul, according to the wisdom given to him, has written to you, as also in all his epistles, speaking in them of these things, in which are some things hard to understand, which untaught and unstable people twist to their own destruction, as they do also the rest of the Scriptures.

~ II Peter 3:15-16

Peter calls Paul's words HARD TO UNDERSTAND and declares them as scriptures. And do you remember what Jesus said to Peter?

I promise you God in heaven will allow whatever you allow on earth, but God will not allow anything you don't allow.

~ Matthew 18:18

Some people use this verse to make Peter a Pope. But Jesus wanted Peter himself to bear witness and declare boldly Paul's writings as scriptures.

If anyone thinks they are a prophet or otherwise gifted by the Spirit, let them acknowledge that what I am writing to you is the Lord's command.

~ 1 Corinthians 14:37

The key to having a uniform interpretation of the Bible in the body of Christ is acknowledging the letters of Paul as the Lord's command.

In all of Paul's letters, he talks about Law vs Grace. This gives us a blueprint on how to go about rightly dividing the word of God. Paul's letters show us the difference between Law and Grace, which produces the right theology.

For example, Under the law (10 commandments), if you keep the laws perfectly you will be blessed. If you break *even one* of the commandments, then you are guilty of breaking all of them. God's fierce anger rests on you and His wrath will hunt your bloodline to the third and fourth generation.

Under the new covenant of Grace God has promised that when we put our *trust in Jesus,* He will never get angry with you nor rebuke you. Because of the perfect work, Jesus did on the Cross, and on account of Him being our advocate at the Father's right hand, we may enter boldly before His Throne.

For this is like the waters of Noah to Me;
For as I have sworn
That the waters of Noah would no longer cover the earth,
So have I sworn
That I would not be angry with you, nor rebuke you.

~ Isaiah 54:9

Preaching that God is still angry at believers is going back to the 10 commandments and is teaching heresy. Discerning Law vs Grace is crucial in understanding the Bible.

7. DISPENSATIONS

Dispensations are different periods or ages in which God deals with mankind differently. Prayer is a perfect topic to demonstrate different dispensations in the Bible. People did not have access to God (prayer) the same way in different dispensations.

Adam spoke to God as though he was next to him. Yet after the fall, God was at a distance. Again, he spoke to Cain when he killed Abel.

Under Noah, (whose name means 'rest' in Hebrew). God seemed to talk to him in his conscious.

During the age of Abraham, it seemed like God talked to Abraham in visions. There were certain discrepancies where Jesus himself came to Abraham in the flesh (Melchizedek coming to Abraham with Bread and Wine).

Again, we see that discrepancy when Jacob wrestles a man (pre-incarnate Jesus), it wasn't the time for Jesus to bless. Yet Jacob fought for it.

God spoke to Joseph in dreams. After a generation of Hebrews who did not know Joseph came in, there was a deafening silence from God until the Children of Israel groaned and God remembered his covenant with Abraham, Isaac and Jacob.

During the time of Moses, there were two dispensations: one before the event of Mount Sinai and another after the 10 commandments were given.

God would be close to the Children of Israel with a cloud for shade by day and pillar of fire by night. But after the 10 commandments were given through Moses. No one could come close to God's presence except Moses.

Under the Law (the 10 commandment and everything that comes with it) access to God was a seriously scary business. Prayer wasn't easy, you had to pray earnestly for long hours and hope God would answer the prayers.

The High Priest would go into the Holy of Holies once a year. If his sins were not atoned for properly, he would be struck dead. They would tie a rope around the Priest's leg so that if he died, they could pull him out without entering God's presence.

The Law and the Prophets were proclaimed until John. Since that time, the good news of the kingdom of God is being preached, and everyone is forcing their way into it.

~ Luke 16:16

This changed everything, the ministry of the law and the prophets were only till the time of John and when the earthly ministry of Jesus began The Lord's Prayer came into effect.
But this prayer was only until the Christ was crucified on the cross, died and rose again. This is the reason you don't find Lord's prayer being prayed by the apostles after the cross. Why?

Remember "forgive us our trespasses, as we forgive those who trespass against us" this has changed after the cross to "Forgive as the Lord forgave you" (Colossians 3:13).

For we are co-workers in God's service; you are God's field, God's building.
~ 1 Corinthians 3:9

Under Grace, we don't pray so that God can be moved but rather we pray because God wants to involve us in HIS works. Make us co-workers in His service. This is why we pray in Tongues.

There will be a time in the future when Jesus rules on Earth, just by thinking things would happen. We will be co-rulers on Earth, 'kings' and Jesus the *King* of Kings.

The method of prayer out of its dispensation or age becomes heresy. Now we are under the Age of Grace. if we go back to the method of approach to God under the law it becomes heresy.

Prayer is not the only thing that changes depending on the age or dispensations. Sometimes, the changes are subtle but have significant results.

For example, Jesus said:

But whosoever shall deny me before men, him will I also deny before my Father which is in heaven.

~ Matthew 10:33

Peter did exactly that.

Then began he to curse and to swear, saying, I know not the man. And immediately the cock crew.

~ Matthew 26:74

Peter denied Jesus with cursing and swearing. You need to imagine Peter using colourful swear words in Aramaic to understand the gravity of the situation.

Jesus ended up giving Peter the responsibility of taking care of his people (Jewish Believers). According to Jesus's own words Jesus should have denied Peter in front of the Father. What happened? Did Jesus lie? What changed?

Judas also betrayed Jesus, felt remorseful and repented.

"I have sinned," he said, "for I have betrayed innocent blood." "What is that to us?" they replied. "That's your responsibility."

~ Matthew 27:4

Both Peter and Judas sinned and repented. Both felt sorry for their actions, but one of them was given the responsibility of feeding God's people and another lost his soul. What happened?

When Peter sinned, he waited for Jesus to pay for his sins while Judas paid for his sin. Peter allowed Jesus to take his sins while Judas pridefully punished himself.

Studying Dispensations in the bible help discern the right theology for the Church. And get us ready for the hope that is to come.

<u>List of Dispensations</u>
Adam
Noah
Abraham
Jacob
Joseph
Moses (Before and after Mount Sinai)
The 10 commandments (David)
John
Jesus's Baptism to The Cross (Jesus's Earthly ministry)
Age of Grace
Before Tribulation and After Tribulation
Age of the kingdom

8. BIBLICAL NAMES

Names are deeply important to human beings, a crucial way of understanding not just the world around us, but each other.

A surname roots us in history and family tradition, while first names establish more identity and personality.

Every name and place in the Bible have a specific meaning. Researching the meaning behind these names can give us tremendous revelations.

Consider the first man we meet in the Bible: Adam. The name "Adam" is so common in Western society now that one might not think to enquire about its meaning.

However, the Hebrew word Adam doesn't simply mean "generic first human" but is rather likely derived from the Hebrew word Adamah meaning 'ground'.

Adam was formed "from the dust of the ground" and so, his name (and the general Hebrew name for 'man') is rooted in how mankind began.

5 Things to Look For in A Biblical Name:

1. God's message.
2. Aspects of a person's birth or the history of a place.
3. A parents' reaction to the birth of their child.
4. The solidarity of family ties
5. Establishes authority over another or indicates a new beginning or new direction in a person's life.

Lots of crucial theologies can be understood by studying names.

Many times, they are illustrations of faith images.

For example Peter, James & John are mentioned many times together in scripture, but if we know the meaning behind their names in Hebrew it gives us a deeper understanding.

Peter: means stones (picture of 10 commandments).
James: in Hebrew means 'supplanted by or replaced by
John: means Grace.

Put them together The 10 commandments (Peter), replaced by (James) Grace (John).

9. BIBLICAL MATHEMATICS

God is an amazing Mathematician. Every number in the Bible has a perfect pattern and every number has a meaning behind it.

The Hebrew language does not have its numbers, instead, it uses the Hebrew Alphabets which has a number attached to each symbol.

Decimal	Hebrew	Glyph	Decimal	Hebrew	Glyph	Decimal	Hebrew	Glyph
1	Aleph	א	10	Yud	י	100	Koof	ק
2	Bet	ב	20	Kaf	כ	200	Reish	ר
3	Gimel	ג	30	Lamed	ל	300	Shin	ש
4	Daleth	ד	40	Mem	מ	400	Taf	ת
5	Heh	ה	50	Nun	נ	500	Kaf(final)	ך
6	Vav	ו	60	Samech	ס	600	Mem(final)	ם
7	Zayin	ז	70	Ayin	ע	700	Nun(final)	ן
8	Het	ח	80	Peh	פ	800	Peh(final)	ף
9	Tet	ט	90	Tzady	צ	900	Tzady(final)	ץ

Study of Biblical Mathematics is called Gematria. God encourages us to find patterns and information in the Bible using numbers.

*Here is wisdom. Let him who has understanding calculate the number of the beast, for it is the number of a man: His number is **666**.*

~ Revelation 13:18

Having $666 as the price of a computer or your door number does

"

not make it a devil's computer nor makes you the antichrist.

In the Bible, every number has a specific meaning.

Number	Meaning	Number	Meaning
1	Unity	7	Completion or Perfection
2	Union or Witness	8	New Beginning
3	Divinity	9	Fruits
4	Earth	10	Law, the 10 commandments
5	Grace	11	Judgment
6	Man	12	Government or dispensations

Number six is the number of men because on the sixth (6th) day the man was made. The number 666, is the number of a man three times in a sequence. Three times speaks of the perversion of men.

Let us have a look at the first sentence of the Old Testament:

"In the beginning, God created the heaven and the earth." GENESIS 1:1

The Hebrew sentence consists of exactly 7 words, which have exactly 28 (4x7) letters. There are 3 nouns: God, heaven and earth. If we add together the numerical value of each of the letters in these three Hebrew nouns, we get exactly 777 (111x7).

The numerical value of the Hebrew word "created" is 203 (29x7). The first three words contain the subject, with exactly 14 (2x7) letters, and the four remaining words contain the object with also exactly 14 letters. The Hebrew words for heaven and earth have 7 letters each.

The value of the first, the two middle and the last letters in the sentence is 133 (19x7). The total value of the first and last letter of every word in the verse is 1,393 (199x7).

The value of the first and last letter of the first and last word in this verse is 497 (71x7). The value of the first and last letter of each word in-between is 896 (128x7).

In this single verse, 30 different options are containing the factor 7. I have only listed 11. The possibility of this all happening by chance is highly impossible.

This is not astrology; we do not use this Bible study tool to predict the future. Gematria has nothing to do with us but to see the beautiful pattern of Jesus Christ and deeper meaning in the bible.

I would advise caution to the reader not to use this tool for fringe pseudo-study like the things of Kabbalah but stick to seeing Jesus in these patterns.

10. THE LAW OF FIRST MENTION

When you find a certain word or passage confusing, often we can gain a better understanding by going to the first time it is mentioned in the Bible. God has designed for us something called "The law of the first mention".

I don't claim to understand why this principle works the way it does. Maybe it has got to do the way God treats first fruits or some other deeper understanding of God.

The principle works such that if we look to the first time a word, topic or a phrase is mentioned, we usually find it's the simplest meaning by reading and examining it. Often, there is also something very significant there that will help you when reading further on.

For example, the first-time blood is mentioned in the Bible is Genesis 4:10, when God asks Cain, "What have you done? Listen! Your brother's blood cries out to me from the ground."

Based on this first mention of blood, we know blood has a voice (information). Modern science caught up recently with the Bible (see forensic science).

to Jesus the mediator of a new covenant, and to the sprinkled blood that speaks a better word than the blood of Abel.

~ Hebrews 12:24

Later we can see that this first mention helps us to understand that Jesus's blood still speaks today.

While Abel's blood cries out for vengeance, Christ's blood shouts out for redemption.

The Law of First Mention brings out accurate interpretation of a topic hence keeping our theologies in check.

11. THE BIBLE INTERPRETING THE BIBLE

While studying the Bible, never look at it from the point of philosophy, previous theologies, emotions, modern culture or any other sources.

Just like we would never use medical science to solve trigonometry problems, we should never use sources outside the Bible to interpret it.

Philosophy, modern culture, human-made theologies or our emotions are sources outside the Biblical narrative using them to interpret the Bible will result in theological fallacies.

For example, when the Bible talks about the Church or Body of Christ, it is speaking of the collective people who believe in the finished works of Christ on the cross.

It has nothing to do with any denomination, building or institution.

Another example would be using Christ's words to Justify or support personal political ideologies.

The whole narrative of the Bible from Genesis to Revelations is about Christ and His finished works on the cross and not a justification of any political ideology anywhere in the world.

The sting of death is sin, and the power of sin is the law.

~ 1 Corinthians 15:56

The law here is not the ceremonial law nor is it the law of the land but the 10 commandments. How do we know this?

I was alive once without the law, but when the commandment came, sin revived and I died. And the commandment, which was to bring life, I found to bring death. For sin, taking occasion by the commandment, deceived me, and by it killed me.

~ Romans 7:9 - 11

Allowing the Bible to interpret itself tears down all bad theologies created by human understanding and interpretation.

12. TYPOLOGY

The study of types and antitypes of Biblical Characters, theology, history, events and statements in the Bible is called Typology. The whole purpose of the Old Testament is viewed as the provision of types for Christ and the fulfilment of the Law.

The most famous types in the bible are the parallel stories of Joseph and Jesus. Both rejected by their Jewish brothers who became the bread of life to the Gentile world, who will one day return for his Jewish brothers.

Typology also teaches us object lessons from the Bible. For instance, the Tree of Knowledge of Good and Evil is equated to the Ten Commandments and the Tree of Life is equated to Christ's works on the Cross. Typology, in this case, teaches us the effects of being under the Tree of Knowledge of Good and Evil versus being under the Tree of Life.

Paul used typology extensively in his letters. He used the Old Testament to preach truths of the New Covenant. He revealed Jesus and His finished works on the cross from the shadows of the Old Testament.

Tell me, you who desire to be under the law, do you not hear the law? For it is written that Abraham had two sons: the one by a bondwoman, the other by a freewoman. But he *who was* of the bondwoman was born according to the flesh, and he of the freewoman through promise, which things are symbolic. For these are the two covenants: the one from Mount Sinai which gives birth to bondage, which is Hagar— for this Hagar is Mount Sinai in Arabia, and corresponds to Jerusalem which now is, and is in bondage with her children— but the Jerusalem above is free, which is the mother of us all.

~ Galatians 4:21-26

Paul equates the Law (Ten Commandments) to Hagar because the Ten Commandments were given to Moses on Mount Sinai. And Paul equates Grace to Sarah because the Holy Spirit was revealed for the first time on mount Zion in Jerusalem.

With this typology, we can go deeper in understanding the quick but temporary effects of the Ten Commandments and the seemingly slow but permanent effects of Grace.

Sarah thought God's promise that she would bear a Son was not enough. She wanted to be practical, so she ordered Abraham to sleep with the servant girl (Hagar).

Sarah and Abraham tried to have a child for years, but were old and still without a child. They got tired of waiting and Abraham decided to sleep with the servant girl ONLY ONCE and Ishmael was born. That was quick.

So the result of preaching the Ten Commandments causes there to be a quick outward result of morality. Whereas Grace seems impractical.

But to what end? Ishmael was such a pain to Sarah that she couldn't stand him. As will be the result of preaching the Ten Commandments. The quick results of outward morality are only temporary. Sarah was so frustrated with Ishmael that she said, "Castaway the bondwoman and her son". So we must also cast away the Ten Commandments, seeing it nailed to Jesus on the cross.

Now we, brethren, as Isaac *was*, are children of promise. But, as he who was born according to the flesh then persecuted him *who was born* according to the Spirit, even so *it is* now. Nevertheless what does the Scripture say? "Cast out the bondwoman and her son, for the son of the bondwoman shall not be heir with the son of the freewoman." So then, brethren, we are not children of the bondwoman but of the free.

~ Galatians 4: 28-31

Overall, Biblical Typology helps believers in many ways. It offers a clear connection between Old and New Testaments, reveals the unity of the Bible, and emphasizes the New Covenant believers experience in the finished work of Jesus Christ.

An understanding of Biblical Typology can help inspire and motivate our faith as we see how God has worked throughout history in profound ways that continue to impact our lives.

13. THE ANSWER IS AT THE GATES

If you don't understand what a certain book of the Bible is talking about, then look for the theme in the very first paragraph of that book.

An interesting phenomenon across all the books of the Bible is that the core theme of the book is seen in the very first paragraph of that book.

For example, in the Book of Genesis, the very first paragraph talks about the beginning, and by this, we understand the Book of Genesis is about Beginnings.

One of the most misinterpreted verses in the Bible is Hebrews 6:4-6.

For *it is* impossible for those who were once enlightened, and have tasted the heavenly gift, and have become partakers of the Holy Spirit, and have tasted the good word of God and the powers of the age to come, if they fall away, to renew them again to repentance, since they crucify again for themselves the Son of God, and put *Him* to an open shame.

~ Hebrews 6:4-6

The verses seem like they say "if you sin wilfully there is no forgiveness" but notice it does not mention sin or sinning. So what is this verse about?

To understand this we need to read the very first chapter of the book and the Title. We know that the book was written to The Hebrews (Πρὸς Ἑβραίους).

This makes it clear that the author was talking to Hebrews who went back to Temple sacrifices after being saved by the Finished Works of Christ on the cross. To them alone, the author says it's impossible to renew them again to repentance.

This is why I titled this Biblical tool as "The Answer is at The Gates". You will find the answers to the core theme of the book, by going back to the beginning of that book.

If a verse is obscure or if it causes misunderstanding, always go back to The Gates for the answers.

The perfect examples of "The Answer is at the Gates" thought process is found in the books of Matthew, Mark, Luke and John.

By reading the very first chapter of each book we find Matthew talks about Kingship of Christ, Mark talks about Christ being the servant, Luke talks about the Humanity of our Savior and John talks about the divinity of Jesus Christ.

14. SEEING JESUS IN EVERY PAGE

This chapter is the crème de la crème of all the tools that can be used to research the Bible. If you forget everything that I've written about, make sure you remember who we discuss here.

Amid the pride, which often can come from intellect and knowledge of researching the bible, *Jesus* is the one seldom discussed.

The Bible, from Genesis to Revelation is about the finished work of Jesus Christ on the cross.

The Key to having a uniform theology in the body of Christ is by having a Spirit of love, but what *is* love?

This is love: not that we loved God, but that he loved us and sent his Son as an atoning sacrifice for our sins.

~ 1 John 4:10

It pleases God when we see and understand His Son's finished work on the cross in the pages of the Bible. This wisdom brings us into uniform theology. It releases us from the restless work of imposing our theology on others in the Church.

The revelation of grace brings true unity to the Body of Christ. Paul talked about this and we all crave to see it and have it. It is not the unity of human theology, of doctrine, rituals, traditions or rules. The unity of God's *love* through Christ Jesus results in right belief, faith, correct theology and a true understanding of the

Word.

A great majority of Christians read the Bible looking for rules and regulations to please God. They read the Bible and see themselves in the pages and stories. Seeing what they are doing right or wrong. This makes an already narcissistic and individualistic human being even more self-centred.

In the beginning, was the Word, and the Word was with God, and the Word was God. He was in the beginning with God. All things were made through Him, and without Him nothing was made that was made.

~ John 1:1-3

Everything in this Universe is created through Christ Jesus. So, it is impossible to truly understand the bible without seeing and focusing on Jesus in its pages.

And beginning with Moses and all the Prophets, he explained to them what was said in all the Scriptures concerning himself.

~ Luke 24:27

Jesus did the same, in the Emmaus road to those two people. He hid their eyes from seeing who he was and showed them about himself from the pages of the Bible.

This tells us one crucial thing that it pleases Jesus that we see him in the pages of the Bible than see him physically.

It is the glory of God to conceal a thing: but the honour of kings is to search out a matter.

~ Proverbs 25:2

God loves to hide truths about Jesus in the Bible. And it's our honour to search it out.

Lot's daughters sleeping with their father, David's general killing David's own Son, King Ahab & Jezebel being eaten by stray dogs, King Jehoram's intestine bursting out.

These events in the Bible make Game of Thrones sound like a Children's Book.

Why is Christendom ashamed to talk about these stories? Why do we never hear preaching from these Biblical events?

These events are not in the Bible to fill the pages. Every word in the Bible is God-breathed, then WHY Do we allow our sense of morality to stop ourselves from being blessed?

The very first thing Jesus did immediately he was raised from the dead was he explained to Two people things from the scriptures about himself.

So, I encourage you, don't be ashamed of these stories and ask the Holy Spirit to show you Jesus himself in these events.